ADVICE

May 12/03

Dear Carolyn,

This is a great little book to refer to now & then — helps keep things in perspective!

Lots of love

David & Margot

SAGE
ADVICE

Lois Kerr

Northstone

Editing: Michael Schwartzentruber, John Sandys-Wunsch
Cover design: Lois Huey-Heck
Consulting art director: Robert MacDonald

Northstone Publishing Inc. is an employee-owned company, committed to caring for the environment and all creation. Northstone recycles, reuses and composts, and encourages readers to do the same. Resources are printed on recycled paper and more environmentally friendly groundwood papers (newsprint), whenever possible. The trees used are replaced through donations to the Scoutrees For Canada Program. Ten percent of all profit is donated to charitable organizations.

Canadian Cataloguing in Publication Data
Kerr, Lois, 1908-
    Sage Advice

    ISBN 1-55145-093-3

    1. Quotations, English. I. Title.

PN6081.K47 1996   082   C96-910351-4

Published by Northstone Publishing Inc.

Northstone

Printed in Canada by Webcom Limited

In Memoriam

This book is dedicated to the memory of
Mollie Cottingham, my mentor and friend.

Mollie encouraged me to write a book that
would be of help in a school system where
values were ignored. Her death prevented
that book from being published; this present
work is a continuation of what she asked for
and I would like it to be a memorial to her
encouragement.

As a solid rock is not shaken by the wind,
wise people falter not amidst blame and
praise.

DHAMMAPADA

Acknowledgments

I would like to thank especially John Sandys-
Wunsch for the work he did editing and producing
the first edition of this book.

Lois Kerr

TABLE OF CONTENTS

What the sages say about...

Addendum

What the sages
say about
the most important
things in life

I have three treasures, which I hold and keep safe: The first is called love, the second is called moderation, the third is called not venturing to go ahead of the world.

THE TAO TE CHING
(Taoist scripture)

Choose always the way that seems the best, however rough it may be. Custom will render it easy and agreeable.

PYTHAGORAS
Ethical Sentences from Strobaeus

Hitch your wagon to a star. Let us not fag in paltry works which serve our pot and bag alone. Let us not lie and steal. Work rather for those interests which the divinities honor and promote – justice, love, freedom, knowledge, utility.

RALPH WALDO EMERSON
Character

I have learned, in whatever state I am, to be content.

SAINT PAUL
Philippians 4:11(RSV)

Happy is anyone who becomes wise
– who comes to have understanding.
There is more profit in it than there is
in silver; it is worth more to you than
gold. Wisdom is more valuable than
jewels; nothing you could want can
compare with it.

HEBREW BIBLE / OLD TESTAMENT
Proverbs 3:13–14 (TEV)

Character is higher than intellect... A
great soul will be strong to live, as
well as to think.

RALPH WALDO EMERSON
The American Scholar

The hell to be endured hereafter, of which theology tells, is no worse than the hell we make for ourselves in this world by habitually fashioning our characters in the wrong way.

WILLIAM JAMES
Psychology, chapter 10

Our life is frittered away by detail. An honest man has hardly need to count more than his ten fingers, or in extreme cases he may add his ten toes, and lump the rest. Simplicity, simplicity, simplicity! I say, let your affairs be as two or three, and not a hundred or a thousand; instead of a million count half a dozen, and keep your accounts on your thumbnail.

HENRY DAVID THOREAU
Walden

What the sages say
about good deeds

Do all the good you can,

By all the means you can,

In all the ways you can,

In all the places you can,

At all the times you can,

To all the people you can,

As long as ever you can.

JOHN WESLEY
His rule

"Is this one of our tribe or a
stranger?" is the question of the
narrow-minded; but to those of a
noble disposition the world is but
one family.

HITOPADESA
(Hindu scripture)

To pity distress is but human; to
relieve it is Godlike.

HORACE MANN
Lectures on Education, Lecture VI

And show kindness unto parents,
and relations, and orphans, and the
poor, and your neighbor who is of
kin to you, and also your neighbor
who is a stranger, and to your famil-
iar companion, and the traveler.

KORAN
Surah 4

At morning, noon, and night, succes-
sively, store up good works.

GAUTAMA
Teaching of Buddha

Strangers who sojourn with you shall be to you as the native-born among you, and you shall love them as yourselves.

HEBREW BIBLE / OLD TESTAMENT
Leviticus 19:34

Everywhere in life, the true question is not what we *gain*, but what we *do*.

THOMAS CARLYLE
Essays, Goethe's Helena

For I was hungry and you gave me food, I was thirsty and you gave me drink, I was a stranger and you welcomed me, I was naked and you clothed me, I was sick and you visited me, I was in prison and you came to me... Truly, I say to you, as you did it to one of the least of these my brothers and sisters, you did it to me.

JESUS
Matthew 25:35–40

What the sages say about making friends

If you would be loved,
love and be lovable.

BENJAMIN FRANKLIN
Poor Richard's Almanack

The only way to have a friend is to be
one.

RALPH WALDO EMERSON
Friendship

For hatred,
friendliness is the antidote.

SIKSHASAMUCCAYA
(Buddhist scripture)

You shall love your neighbor
as yourself.

JESUS
Matthew 22:39 (RSV)

It does not greatly concern me that people do not know me; my great concern is my not knowing them.

CONFUCIUS
The Analects

The person who is naturally in sympathy with others, to that person will all others come.

CHUANG-TZU
The Writings of Chuang-Tzu

As your life is dear to yourself, so also are the lives of all beings. The good show compassion towards all living beings because of their resemblance to themselves.

THE HITOPADESA
(Hindu scripture)

People who expel malice from their own heart find the whole creation their friend.

ASTAPADI
(Sikh scripture) 3; Pauri 6

One who forgives an offense fosters friendship, but one who dwells on disputes will alienate a friend.

HEBREW BIBLE /OLD TESTAMENT
Proverbs 17:9 (NRSV)

Confucius said, "There are three sorts of friend that are profitable, and three sorts that are harmful. Friendship with the upright, with the true-to-death, and with those who have heard much is profitable. Friendship with the obsequious, friendship with those who are good at accommodating their principles, friendship with those who are clever at talk is harmful."

CONFUCIUS
The Analects

What the sages say
about standing up
to the crowd

_____

Is it so bad then to be misunderstood? Pythagoras was misunderstood, and Socrates, and Jesus, and Luther, and Copernicus, and Galileo, and Newton, and every pure and wise spirit that ever took flesh. To be great is to be misunderstood.

RALPH WALDO EMERSON
Essays: Self Reliance

For how many things, which for our own sake we should never do, do we perform for the sake of our friends?

CICERO
De Amicitia, 16

A wicked person who reproaches a virtuous person is like one who looks up and spits at heaven; the spittle soils not heaven, but comes back and defiles the one who spat.

GAUTAMA
The Sutra of the Forty-two Sections

Happy are those who reject the advice of evil people, who do not follow the example of sinners or join those who have no use for God.

HEBREW BIBLE / OLD TESTAMENT
Psalm 1:1 (TEV)

The mind is lowered through association with inferiors. With equals it attains equality, and with superiors, superiority.

THE HITOPADESA
(Hindu scripture)

It is easy in the world to live after the world's opinion; it is easy in solitude to live after our own; but the great man is he who in the midst of the crowd keeps with perfect sweetness the independence of solitude.

RALPH WALDO EMERSON
Character

Haven't you ever read what the Scriptures say? "The stone which the builders rejected as worthless turned out to be the most important of all."

JESUS
Matthew 21:42 (TEV)

If a man does not keep pace with his companions, perhaps it is because he hears a different drummer. Let him step to the music which he hears, however measured or far away.

HENRY DAVID THOREAU
Walden

What the sages say
about telling the truth

Tell the truth, but pleasantly and gently. Do not tell it rudely, for truth-telling that hurts and repels does not carry conviction.

THE LAWS OF MANU
(Hindu scripture)

Whatsoever is not said in all sincerity, is wrongly said.

CHUANG-TZU
The Writings of Chuang-Tzu

So then, putting away falsehood, let all of us speak the truth to our neighbors, for we are members one of another.

SAINT PAUL
Ephesians 4:25 (NRSV)

Be true and honest in all you say, and seriously earnest in all you do, and then, even if your country be one inhabited by barbarians, South or North, you will make your way.

CONFUCIUS
The Analects

Woe unto each sinful liar.

KORAN
Surah 45

An honest man's the noblest work of God.

ALEXANDER POPE
Essay on Man Ep. 1, 1.247

It is not without good reason said,
that he who has not a good memory
should never take upon him the
trade of lying.

MICHEL DE MONTAIGNE
Essays: Of Liars

What the sages say about keeping laws and rules

The world stands upon three things:
upon the Law, upon worship, and
upon showing kindness.

MISHNAH
Tractate Aboth 1:2

Just laws are no restraint upon the
freedom of the good, for the good
desire nothing which a just law will
interfere with.

J.A. FROUDE
*Short Studies on Great Subjects: Reciprocal Duties of
State and Subject*

The law is the last result of human wisdom acting upon human experience for the benefit of the public.

SAMUEL JOHNSON
Piozzi's Anecdotes

The person who obeys with modesty appears worthy of someday or other being allowed to command.

CICERO
On the Laws

Where law ends, there tyranny
begins.

WILLIAM PITT THE ELDER
(EARL OF CHATHAM)
Case of Wilkes (Speech), Jan. 9, 1770

There is a higher law than the Consti-
tution.

W.H. SEWARD
(Speech), Mar. 11, 1850

What the sages say
about good manners

Life is not so short but that there is
always time enough for courtesy.

RALPH WALDO EMERSON
Social Aims

Let superior persons keep watch
over themselves without ceasing,
showing deference to others, with
propriety of manners... and all within
the four seas will be their allies.

CONFUCIUS
The Analects

How sweet and gracious, even in
common speech,
Is that fine sense which men call
Courtesy!
Wholesome as air and genial as the
light,
Welcome in every clime as breath of
flowers,
It transmutes aliens into trusting
friends,
And gives its owner passport round
the globe.

JAMES T. FIELDS
Courtesy

You shall rise before the aged, and
defer to the old.

HEBREW BIBLE /OLD TESTAMENT
Leviticus 19:32 (NRSV)

Manners aim to facilitate life, to get rid
of impediments... They aid our deal-
ings and conversation, as a railway
aids traveling, by getting rid of all
avoidable obstructions of the road.

RALPH WALDO EMERSON
Manners

In conversation, avoid the extremes
of forwardness and reserve.

CATO
Maxims

Do not find fault before you investi-
gate; first consider and then reprove.
Do not answer before you have
heard, nor interrupt people before
they finish.
Do not argue about a matter which
does not concern you, nor sit with
sinners when they judge a case.

APOCRYPHA
Ecclesiasticus 11:7–9

What the sages say about pride and humility

Pride goes before destruction, and a
haughty spirit before a fall.

HEBREW BIBLE / OLD TESTAMENT
Proverbs 16:18 (NRSV)

In general, pride is at the bottom of
all great mistakes.

JOHN RUSKIN
Conceptions of God

Superior people are modest in their words, profuse in their deeds.

CONFUCIUS
The Analects

For those who make themselves great will be humbled, and those who humble themselves will be made great.

JESUS
Luke 18:14 (TEV)

But many who are first will be last;
and the last will be first.

JESUS
Mark 10:31 (NRSV)

Let another praise you, and not your
own mouth – a stranger, and not
your own lips.

HEBREW BIBLE / OLD TESTAMENT
Proverbs 27:2 (NRSV)

It is in general more profitable to
reckon up our defects than to boast
of our attainments.

THOMAS CARLYLE
Essays: Signs of the Times

Walk not proudly in the land, for you
cannot cleave the earth, neither can
you equal the mountains in stature.

KORAN
Surah 17

Be not arrogant because of that
which you know; deal with the
ignorant as with the learned.

PTAH-HOTEP
The Book of Ptah-Hotep

Persons of superior virtue are not
conscious of their virtue, and in this
way they possess virtue.
Persons of inferior virtue never lose
sight of their virtue, and in this way
lose their virtue...

TAO TE CHING
(Taoist scripture) 38

Humility, like darkness, reveals the heavenly lights.

HENRY DAVID THOREAU
Walden

What the sages say about bridling the tongue

Kind words are like honey – sweet to
the taste and good for your health.

HEBREW BIBLE / OLD TESTAMENT
Proverbs 16:24 (TEV)

Your evil thoughts and evil words
hurt only yourself and not another.

GAUTAMA
Life of Buddha

It is not what goes into your mouth
that makes you ritually unclean;
rather, what comes out of it makes
you unclean.

JESUS
Matthew 15:11 (TEV)

You shall not bear false witness
against your neighbor.

HEBREW BIBLE / OLD TESTAMENT
Exodus 20:16 (NRSV)

Do not use my name for evil purposes, because I, the Lord your God, will punish anyone who misuses my name.

HEBREW BIBLE / OLD TESTAMENT
Exodus 20:7 (TEV)

May my words and my thoughts be acceptable to you, O Lord, my refuge and my redeemer.

HEBREW BIBLE / OLD TESTAMENT
Psalm 19:14 (TEV)

Leave the sins of the tongue, and
practice virtue with thy tongue.

DHAMMAPADA
(Buddhist scripture) 17:232

Woe to every slanderer and backbiter.

KORAN
Surah 104

Without wood, a fire goes out;
without gossip, quarreling ceases.

HEBREW BIBLE / OLD TESTAMENT
Proverbs 26:20

But no one has ever been able to tame the tongue. It is evil and uncontrollable, full of deadly poison. We use it to give thanks to our Lord and God and also to curse our neighbor, who is created in the likeness of God. Words of thanksgiving and cursing pour out from the same mouth. My friends, this should not happen. No spring of water pours out sweet water and bitter water from the same opening.

NEW TESTAMENT
James 3:8-11

After all, even fools may be thought
wise and intelligent if they stay quiet
and keep their mouths shut.

HEBREW BIBLE / OLD TESTAMENT
Proverbs 17:28 (TEV)

Do not speak harshly to anyone; those
who are spoken to will answer you in
the same way. Angry speech is pain-
ful; blows for blows will touch you.

DHAMMAPADA
(Buddhist scripture) 10:133

You who spend your time discussing the good and bad qualities of others waste your time. For it is time spent neither in thinking about your own self nor of the Supreme Self, but of other selves.

RAMAKRISHNA
Sayings of Ramakrishna

The slanderer is like one who flings dust at another when the wind is contrary; the dust returns to the one who threw it.

GAUTAMA
The Sutra of the Forty-two Sections

Gossip is the sort of smoke that comes from the dirty tobacco pipes of those who diffuse it; it proves nothing but the bad taste of the smoker.

GEORGE ELIOT
Daniel Deronda, Book 11, chap. 13

Keep to yourself any knowledge that may prove unpleasant, till someone else has disclosed it... Bring, O nightingale! the glad tidings of the spring, and leave the owl to be the harbinger of evil.

SA'DI
The Gulistan

What the sages say
about anger

Thou shalt not kill.

HEBREW BIBLE / OLD TESTAMENT
Exodus 20:13 (KJV)

The start of an argument is like the first break in a dam; stop it before it goes any further.

HEBREW BIBLE / OLD TESTAMENT
Proverbs 17:14 (TEV)

Anger! how it changes the comely face,
how it destroys the loveliness of
beauty! Anger dulls the brightness of
the eye, chokes all desire to hear the
principles of truth, cuts and divides the
principle of family affection, impover-
ishes and weakens every worldly aim.
Therefore let anger be subdued, yield
not to the angry impulse.

GAUTAMA
Life of Buddha

Hatred is increased through return of
hatred, but may be destroyed by love.

BARUCH SPINOZA
Ethics

Don't give in to worry or anger; it
only leads to trouble.

HEBREW BIBLE / OLD TESTAMENT
Psalms 37:8 (TEV)

People with a hot temper do foolish things; wiser people remain calm.

HEBREW BIBLE / OLD TESTAMENT
Proverbs 14:17 (TEV)

Nothing will protect us from external compulsion so much as the control of ourselves.

ARTHUR SCHOPENHAUER
Counsels and Maxims

So if you are about to offer your gift
to God at the altar and there you
remember that your neighbor has
something against you, leave your
gift there in front of the altar, go at
once and make peace with your
neighbor, and then come back and
offer your gift to God.

JESUS
Matthew 5:23–25

For they sow the wind, and they
shall reap the whirlwind.

HEBREW BIBLE / OLD TESTAMENT
Hosea 8:7 (RSV)

It is wrong to get into a passion with one's neighbors, to be no longer master of one's words.

PTAH-HOTEP
The Book of Ptah-Hotep

By the fact of their not remembering old grievances, they gradually did away with resentment.

CONFUCIUS
The Analects

Do not take revenge on someone
who wrongs you. If anyone slaps you
on the right cheek, let that person
slap your left cheek too.

JESUS
Matthew 4:39

With the conquest of my mind, I
have conquered the whole world.

ADI GRANTH
(Sikh scripture) Japuji 20

Though they should conquer a million warriors on the battlefield, yet indeed, the noblest victors are those who have conquered themselves.

DHAMMAPADA
(Buddhist scripture) 8:103

It is better to be patient than power-ful. It is better to win control over yourself than over whole cities.

HEBREW BIBLE / OLD TESTAMENT
Proverbs 16:32 (TEV)

Attack the evil that is within yourself;
do not attack the evil that is in others.

CONFUCIUS
The Analects

It is true that the mind is restless and difficult to control. But it can be conquered, Arjuna, through regular practice and detachment. Those who lack self-control will find it difficult to progress in meditation; but those who are self-controlled, striving earnestly through the right means, will attain the goal.

BHAGAVAD-GITA
(Hindu scripture) 6,35–36

What the sages say
about the mind

It is the mind that makes one wise or
ignorant, bound or emancipated.
One is holy because of the mind, one
is wicked because of the mind, one is
a sinner because of the mind, and it
is the mind that makes one virtuous.

RAMAKRISHNA
The Sayings of Ramakrishna

Be careful how you think; your life is
shaped by your thoughts.

HEBREW BIBLE / OLD TESTAMENT
Proverbs 4:23 (TEV)

Fill your minds with those things
that are good and that deserve
praise: things that are true, noble,
right, pure, lovely, and honorable.

SAINT PAUL
Philippians 4:8 (TEV)

Strength of mind is exercise, not rest.

ALEXANDER POPE
Essay on Man, Ep. II, L. 104

Our mind acts at times and at times suffers; in so far as it has adequate ideas, it necessarily acts; and in so far as it has inadequate ideas, it necessarily suffers.

BARUCH SPINOZA
Ethics

The mind is its own place, and in itself can make a heaven of hell, a hell of heaven.

JOHN MILTON
Paradise Lost, Book 1

A sound Mind in a sound Body, is a short but full description of a happy State in this World.

JOHN LOCKE
Thoughts Concerning Education

It is good to tame the mind, which is difficult to hold in and flighty, rushing wherever it will; a tamed mind brings happiness.

DHAMMAPADA
(Buddhist scripture) 3:35

What the sages say about getting an education

Learning, without thought, is a snare;
thought, without learning, is a danger.

CONFUCIUS
The Analects

There is no greater wealth than
wisdom; no greater poverty than
ignorance; no greater heritage than
culture.

NAHJUL BALAGHA
(Shiite Islam writing) Saying 52

We should treat our minds, that is, ourselves, as innocent and ingenuous children, whose guardians we are, and be careful what objects and what subjects we thrust on their attention. Read not the *Times*. Read the *Eternities*.

HENRY DAVID THOREAU
Walden

Knowledge is power.

FRANCIS BACON
Meditations sacrae

Knowledge is, indeed, that which,
next to virtue, truly and essentially
raises one above another.

JOSEPH ADDISON
The Guardian. Letter of Alexander to Aristotle, iii

Learning imparts a heightened
charm to a homely face. Knowledge
is the best treasure that a person can
secretly hoard up in life.

GARUDA PURANA
(Hindu scripture)

All that we are is the result of what we have thought; it is founded in our thoughts, it is made up of our thoughts. If a person speaks or acts with an evil thought, pain will follow... If a person speaks or acts with a pure thought, happiness will follow.

DHAMMAPADA
(Buddhist scripture) 1:1

If time is precious, no book that will not improve by repeated readings deserves to be read at all.

THOMAS CARLYLE
Essays: Goethe's Helena

Finally, education alone can conduct
us to that enjoyment which is, at once,
best in quality and infinite in quantity.

HORACE MANN
Lectures and reports on education, Lecture 1

When Confucius was going to Wei, Jan Ch'iu drove him. The Master said, "What a dense population!" Jan Ch'iu said, "When the people have multiplied, what next should be done for them?" The Master said, "Enrich them." Jan Ch'iu said, "When one has enriched them, what next should be done for them?" The Master said, "Instruct them."

CONFUCIUS
The Analects

What the sages say
about sexual passions

Chastity is the cement of civilization
and progress.

MARY BAKER EDDY
Science and Health

Nothing hinders the perception of
truth more than a life devoted to lusts.

SAINT AUGUSTINE
Of True Religion

As a fierce fire excited from within a house, so is the fire of covetous desire; the burning flare of covetous desire is fiercer far than fire which burns the world. For fire may be put out by water in excess, but what can overpower the fire of lust?

GAUTAMA
Teachings of Buddha

But I say, walk by the Spirit, and do not gratify the desires of the flesh. For the desires of the flesh are against the Spirit, and the desires of the Spirit are against the flesh; for these are opposed to each other, to prevent you from doing what you would.

SAINT PAUL
Galatians 5:16–17 (RSV)

Peace of mind makes the body healthy, but jealousy is like a cancer.

HEBREW BIBLE / OLD TESTAMENT
Proverbs 14:30 (RSV)

Chastity is the flowering of man; and what are called Genius, Heroism, Holiness, and the like, are but various fruits which succeed it. Man flows at once to God when the channel of purity is open.

HENRY DAVID THOREAU
Walden

What the sages say
about marriage

The family is the avenue of human perpetuity... it could carry on the race even if all other institutions failed.

GEORGE SANTAYANA
Reason in Society

I'd place more faith in a love that resulted from marriage than in a marriage that resulted from love.

RICHARD J. NEEDHAM
from a column in the Toronto Globe and Mail

If a man divorces his wife, the altar
itself sheds tears over him.

TALMUD

Let there be mutual fidelity ending in
death alone; this, in short, should be
acknowledged as the highest law of
duty for man or wife.

THE LAWS OF MANU
(Hindu scripture)

Thou shalt not commit adultery.

HEBREW BIBLE / OLD TESTAMENT
Exodus 20:14 (KJV)

Can you carry fire against your chest without burning your clothes? Can you walk on hot coals without burning your feet? It is just as dangerous to sleep with another person's spouse. Whoever does it will suffer.

HEBREW BIBLE / OLD TESTAMENT
Proverbs 6:27–29

You have heard that it was said, "Do not commit adultery." But now I tell you; anyone who looks at a woman and wants to possess her is guilty of committing adultery with her in his heart.

JESUS
Matthew 5:27–28 (TEV)

Thus grief still treads upon the heels of pleasure;
Married in haste, we may repent at leisure

WILLIAM CONGREVE
The Old Bachelor, Act 5, Sc. 1

Any marriage based on physical
attraction alone is doomed to failure.

BILLY GRAHAM
speaking at a crusade in Arizona August 27, 1974

What the sages say
about the relationship
between parents and
their children

Honor your father and your mother;
that your days may be long in the
land that the Lord your God is
giving you.

HEBREW BIBLE / OLD TESTAMENT
Exodus 20:12 (NRSV)

You must think of your ancestors and
continue to cultivate the virtue which
you inherit from them.

CONFUCIUS
The Book of Filial Duty

Correction and discipline are good for children. If they have their own way, they will make their mothers ashamed of them.

HEBREW BIBLE / OLD TESTAMENT
Proverbs 29:15 (TEV)

Children, obey your parents in the Lord, for this is right.

SAINT PAUL
Ephesians 6:1 (RSV)

Respect women who have borne you.

KORAN
Surah 4

The tender bamboo can be easily
bent, but the full-grown bamboo
breaks when attempt is made to bend
it. It is easy to bend young hearts
toward God...

RAMAKRISHNA
The Sayings of Ramakrishna

My child, keep your father's commandment, and do not forsake your mother's teaching. Bind them upon your heart always; tie them about your neck. When you walk, they will lead you; when you lie down, they will watch over you; and when you awake, they will talk with you.

HEBREW BIBLE / OLD TESTAMENT
Proverbs 6:20–22 (RSV)

When the command is wrong, a child should resist the parent.

CONFUCIUS
The Book of Filial Duty

What the sages say
about work

To labor is to pray.
(*Laborare est orare.*)

BENEDICTINE MONKS
motto

Women, as well as men, can only
find their identity in work that uses
their full capacities.

BETTY FRIEDAN
The Feminine Mystique

"Whoever refuses to work is not allowed to eat." We say this because we hear that there are some people among you who live lazy lives and who do nothing except meddle in other people's business.

SAINT PAUL
2 Thessalonians 3:10–11 (TEV)

Do not hire a person who does your work for money, but one who does it for love of it.

HENRY DAVID THOREAU
Life Without Principle

Go to the ant, you lazybones, consider its ways, and be wise. Without having any chief or officer or ruler, it prepares its food in summer, and gathers its sustenance in harvest. How long will you lie there, O lazybones? When will you rise from your sleep? A little sleep, a little slumber, a little folding of the hands to rest, and poverty will come upon you like a robber, and want like an armed warrior.

HEBREW BIBLE / OLD TESTAMENT
Proverbs 6:6–11 (NRSV)

Something attempted,
something done,
Has earned a night's repose.

HENRY WADSWORTH LONGFELLOW
The Village Blacksmith

You have never done enough, so long
as it is still possible that you have
something of value to contribute.

DAG HAMMARSKJÖLD
Markings

No labor, however humble,
is dishonoring.

TALMUD
Gemara, Nedarim

The importance of nations lies in
work – work in the field, work in the
vineyards, work with the loom, work
in the tannery, work in the quarry,
work in the lumberyard, work in the
office and in the press.

KAHLIL GIBRAN
Spiritual Sayings of Kahlil Gibran

I wish to preach not the doctrine of ignoble ease, but the doctrine of the strenuous life.

THEODORE ROOSEVELT
speech, 1899

I propose to tell you the secret of life as I have seen the game played, and as I have tried to play it myself... Though a little one, the master-word looms large in meaning. It is the open sesame to every portal, the great equalizer in the world, the true philosopher's stone which transmutes all the base metal of humanity into gold. The stupid among you it will make bright, the bright brilliant, and the brilliant steady. With the magic word in your heart all things are possible, and without it all study is vanity and vexation... And the Master-Word is Work... write it on the tables of your heart, and bind it upon your forehead.

SIR WILLIAM OSLER
The Master-word in Medicine, address to students in Toronto, 1903

What the sages say
about wealth and
material possessions

Man's value is in the few things he
creates and not in the many possessions he amasses.

KAHLIL GIBRAN
Spiritual Sayings of Kahlil Gibran

It is better to contract yourself within
the compass of a small fortune and
be happy, than to have a great one
and be wretched.

EPICTETUS
Discourses

What a man *is* contributes more to his happiness than what he has.

SCHOPENHAUER
Counsels and Maxims

To take to oneself unrighteous wealth is like satisfying one's hunger with putrid food, or one's thirst with poison wine. It gives a temporary relief, indeed, but death also follows it.

TREATISE ON RESPONSE AND RETRIBUTION
(Taoist scripture) 5

Do not save riches here on earth,
where moths and rust destroy, and
robbers break in and steal. Instead,
save riches in heaven, where moths
and rust cannot destroy, and robbers
cannot break in and steal. For your
heart will always be where your
riches are.

JESUS
Matthew 6:19–21 (TEV)

And whoso is saved from his own
greed, such are the successful.

KORAN
Surah 64

The foolish by their thirst for riches
destroy themselves.

DHAMMAPADA
(Buddhist scripture) 24:355

Superfluous wealth can buy
superfluities only. Money is not
required to buy one necessary (thing)
of the soul.

HENRY DAVID THOREAU
Walden

Where there is habitual going after
gain, there is much ill will.

CONFUCIUS
The Analects

My father taught that all people, no matter what their situation, were to be treated alike. He would say: "My son, when a man passes in his canoe, if you are too poor to offer him bread, call him in anyway to rest, and to share the warmth of your fire." How much more beautiful can life be?

It is that belief which has been lost; that life is to share - not to acquire. As we shared, so people respected us. You. The more you have, the more you take, in order to show in worldly possessions what you command... Because you do not want nature. You want Something that belongs to you; I put it there; you can't have it.

And the white man accuses the Indian of living for the day! We did not, not ever. We live for centuries ahead. You are the people who live for the day, destroying wherever you go. You do not worry about your grandchildren and how they will live...

The white world is producing very smart, stereotyped non-humans who have lost their feeling, not just for other humans, but for all living things. Your whole life meaning is to be on top of the other person.

GEORGE CLUTESI
from an interview with Hilda Mortimer in the Montreal Star, Aug. 9, 1969

What the sages say
about stealing

Thou shalt not steal.

HEBREW BIBLE / OLD TESTAMENT
Exodus 20:15 (KJV)

Robbers love their own homes but not the homes of others, so they rob other homes in order to benefit their own... If all through the world people will regard the families of others as their own, who will then rob, steal, or disturb?

MO-TI
Essays

He that steals an egg will steal an ox.

GEORGE HERBERT
Jacula Prudentum

The way of universal love and mutual aid... is to regard the state of others as one's own, the houses of others as one's own, the persons of others as one's self.

MO-TI
Essays

That nature alone is good which refrains from doing unto another whatsoever is not good for itself.

ZOROASTER
Dadistan-I-Dinik, 94.5

What the sages say
about drinking

What is life worth without wine? It was created to make people happy. Drunk at the right time and in the right amount, wine makes for a glad heart and a cheerful mind. Bitterness of soul comes from wine drunk to excess, out of temper, or bravado. Drunkenness excites the stupid to a fury to their own harm, it reduces their strength while leading to blows.

APOCRYPHA
Ecclesiasticus 31:27-30 (NJB)

Don't associate with people who drink too much wine or stuff themselves with food. Drunkards and gluttons will be reduced to poverty. If all you do is eat and sleep, you will soon be wearing rags.

HEBREW BIBLE / OLD TESTAMENT
Proverbs 23:20-21 (TEV)

However, you may comfort yourself
by being assured that we are not
drinking water, but have plenty of
good beer and Rhenish wine, with
which we cheer ourselves in spite of
the overflowing river.

MARTIN LUTHER
(1483-1546) in a letter to his wife

Satan only desires to precipitate
enmity and hatred between you in
regard to wine and arrow-shuffling,
and to bar you from the remem-
brance of God, and from prayer. Will
you then desist?

KORAN
Surah 5

Of eight things a little is good and
much is evil: travel, mating, wealth,
work, wine, sleep, spiced drinks, and
medicine.

TALMUD
Gemara, Gittin 70

That inasmuch as any person drinks wine or strong drink among you, behold it is not good.

DOCTRINE AND COVENANTS
(Mormon Religion) 89.5, 7-9

I am glad to have drunk water so long, for the same reason that I prefer the natural sky to an opium-eater's heaven. I would fain keep sober always; and there are infinite degrees of drunkenness. I believe that water is the only drink for a wise man.

HENRY DAVID THOREAU
Walden

What sages say
about leaders

Let leaders show rectitude in their own personal character, and even without directions from them things will go well. If they be not personally upright, their directions will not be complied with.

CONFUCIUS
The Analects

Whatever a great person does, ordinary people will imitate; they follow the person's example.

BHAGAVAD-GITA
(Hindu scripture)

When you are at the head of the city,
know how not to take advantage of
the fact that you have reached the
first rank, harden not your heart
because of your elevation; you have
become only the steward of the good
things of God.

PTAH-HOTEP
The Book of Ptah-Hotep

Exhibit true superiority by virtuous
conduct and the highest exercise of
reason.

GAUTAMA
Life of Buddha

As the magistrate is, so will the magistrate's officials be; as the governor of the city is, so will the inhabitants of the city be.

APOCRYPHA
Ecclesiasticus 10:2

Let a ruler govern upon virtuous principles, and this ruler will be like the pole-star, which remains steadfast in its place, while all the host of stars turn towards it.

CONFUCIUS
The Analects

The one who is greatest among you
shall be your servant; all who exalt
themselves will be humbled, and all
who humble themselves will be
exalted.

JESUS
Matthew 23:11–12 (AILL)

Men of character are the conscience
of the society to which they belong.

RALPH WALDO EMERSON
Character

The heights by great men reached
and kept
Were not attained by sudden flight,
But they, while their companions
slept,
Were toiling upward in the night.

HENRY WADSWORTH LONGFELLOW
Birds of Passage, The Ladder of St. Augustine, St. 10

Patience is a necessary ingredient of
genius.

BENJAMIN DISRAELI
Contarini Fleming, Pt. IV, Ch. V

Sit in the assembly of the honest; join
with those that are good and virtuous; nay, seek out a noble enemy
where enmity cannot be helped and
have nothing to do with the wicked
and the unrighteous. Even in bond-
age you should live with the virtuous, the erudite, and the truthful; but
not for a kingdom should you stay
with the wicked and the malicious.

GARUDA PURANA
(Hindu scripture) 112

O ye kind heavens! there is in every nation... a fittest, a wisest, bravest, best; whom could we find and make king over us... By what art discover him? For our need of him is great!

THOMAS CARLYLE
Past and Present

What the sages say
about the wise and
the foolish,
about wisdom
and folly

What is the part of wisdom? To dream with one eye open; to be detached from the world without being hostile to it; to welcome fugitive beauties and pity fugitive sufferings, without forgetting for a moment how fugitive they are.

GEORGE SANTAYANA
Reason and Society

For the price of wisdom is above rubies.

HEBREW BIBLE / OLD TESTAMENT
Job 28:18 (KJV)

For the heart of the wise is in the house of mourning; but the heart of fools is in the house of mirth.

HEBREW BIBLE / OLD TESTAMENT
Ecclesiastes 7:4 (NRSV)

Come look at this world, glittering like a royal chariot; the foolish are immersed in it, but the wise do not touch it.

DHAMMAPADA
(Buddhist scripture) 13:171

Again, the kingdom of heaven is like
a merchant in search of fine pearls;
who, on finding one pearl of great
value, went and sold everything and
bought it.

JESUS
Matthew 13:45–46 (AILL)

As a solid rock is not shaken by the
wind, wise people falter not amidst
blame and praise.

DHAMMAPADA
(Buddhist scripture) 6:81

Let no one think lightly of good,
saying, it will not come nigh unto
me. Even by the falling of water
drops, a water pot is filled; the wise
become full of good, even if they
gather it little by little.

DHAMMAPADA
(Buddhist scripture) 9:12

A grain of gold will gild a great
surface, but not so much as a grain of
wisdom.

HENRY DAVID THOREAU
Walden

Wise people, after they have listened
to the laws, become serene, like a
deep, smooth, and still lake.

DHAMMAPADA
(Buddhist scripture) 6:82

Well-makers lead the water wherever
they like; fletchers bend the arrow;
carpenters bend a log of wood; wise
people fashion themselves.

DHAMMAPADA
(Buddhist scripture) 6:80

Infinitely quiet is the place where the wise find their abode; no need of arms or weapons there! Subdued the power of covetous desire and angry thoughts and ignorance, there's nothing left in the wide world to conquer!

DHAMMAPADA
(Buddhist scripture) 4:12

For fools rush in where angels fear to tread.

ALEXANDER POPE
Essay on Criticism, Pt. III, L. 66

Across the sea of birth and death,
"wisdom" is the handy bark; "wisdom" is the shining lamp that light-
ens up the dark and gloomy world.
Wisdom is the grateful medicine for
all the defiling ills of life; wisdom is
the ax wherewith to level all the
tangled forest of ignorance and lust -
therefore, in every way, by thought
and right attention, people should
diligently work to engender wisdom.

DHAMMAPADA
(Buddhist scripture) 7:18

As... the lion, king of beasts, is reckoned chief among animals, for its strength, speed, and bravery, so is the faculty of wisdom reckoned chief among mental states helpful to enlightenment.

BUDDHIST PROVERB

Fools show their anger at once, but the prudent ignore an insult.

HEBREW BIBLE / OLD TESTAMENT
Proverbs 12:16 (RSV)

Happy is anyone who becomes wise
– who comes to have understanding.
There is more profit in it than there is
in silver; it is worth more than gold.
Wisdom is more valuable than
jewels; nothing you could want can
compare with it. Wisdom offers you
long life, as well as wealth and
honor. Wisdom can make your life
pleasant and lead you safely through
it. Those who become wise are
happy; wisdom will give them life.

HEBREW BIBLE / OLD TESTAMENT
Proverbs 3:13–18, (TEV)

Only the wise know what things really mean. Wisdom makes them smile and makes their frown disappear.

HEBREW BIBLE / OLD TESTAMENT
Ecclesiastes 8:1 (TEV)

To fear the Lord is the beginning of wisdom.

APOCRYPHA
Ecclesiasticus 1:14 (RSV)

Rabbi Jose ben Kisma said:

"There are seven traits of the wise:

They do not speak in the presence of those wiser than themselves;

They do not interrupt when a colleague speaks;

They do not rush out with a rejoinder;

They ask questions that are relevant, and give answers that are logical;

They deal with first things first and last things last;

They readily admit when they do not know about a matter;

They acknowledge the truth.

The opposites of these traits mark the boorish."

TALMUD
Mishnah, Aboth

Those fools who know their foolish-
ness, are wise at least so far. But fools
who think themselves wise, they are
called fools indeed.

DHAMMAPADA
(Buddhist scripture) 5:63

As a vessel is known by the sound,
whether it be cracked or not; so
people are proved, by their speeches,
whether they be wise or foolish.

DEMOSTHENES

When a youth was taking on airs in the theater and saying, "I am wise, for I have conversed with many wise people," Epictetus replied, "I too have conversed with many rich people, yet I am not rich!"

EPICTETUS
Sayings, 65

Fools think their own way is right, but the wise listen to advice.

HEBREW BIBLE / OLD TESTAMENT
Proverbs 12:15 (NRSV)

When the learned drive away vanity
by earnestness, they, the wise, climb-
ing the terraced heights of wisdom,
look down upon the fools; free from
sorrow they look upon the sorrowing
crowd, as those that stand on a
mountain look down upon them that
stand upon the plain.

DHAMMAPADA
(Buddhist scripture) 2:28

If you desire wisdom, keep the
commandments.

APOCRYPHA
Ecclesiasticus 1:26 (RSV)

A fool takes no pleasure in understanding, but only in expressing
personal opinion.

HEBREW BIBLE / OLD TESTAMENT
Proverbs 18:2 (NRSV)

All wisdom comes from the Lord,

and it is with the Lord for ever.

The sand of the sea, the drops of rain,

and the days of eternity –

who can assess them?

The height of heaven, the breadth of

the earth,

the abyss, and wisdom –

who can search them out?

Wisdom was created before all

things,

And prudent understanding from

eternity.

APOCRYPHA
Ecclesiasticus 1:1–4

Those who make wealth their all in all, cannot bear loss of money. Those who make distinction their all in all, cannot bear loss of fame. Those who affect power will not place authority in the hands of others. Anxious while holding, distressed if losing, yet never taking warning from the past and seeing the folly of their pursuit – such are those accursed of God.

CHUANG TZU
Sayings of Chuang Tzu

What the sages say
about superior
and inferior people

When you meet with those of worth,
think how you may attain to their
level; when you see others of an
opposite character, look within, and
examine yourself.

CONFUCIUS
The Analects

Those of superior mind are placidly
composed; the small-minded are in a
constant state of perturbation.

CONFUCIUS
The Analects

The noble-minded make the most of others' good qualities, not the worst of their bad ones. Those of small mind do the reverse of this.

CONFUCIUS
The Analects

The nobler-minded will be agreeable even when they disagree; the small-minded will agree and be disagreeable.

CONFUCIUS
The Analects

Those of superior mind busy themselves first in getting at the root of things.

CONFUCIUS
The Analects

Superior persons are exacting on themselves; common persons are exacting of others.

CONFUCIUS
The Analects

The superior person may not be conversant with petty details, and yet may be responsible for important matters. The inferior person may not be charged with important matters, yet may be conversant with the petty details.

CONFUCIUS
The Analects

This world is not for those who doth not worship.

HENRY DAVID THOREAU
Walden

There are nine things of which the
superior person should be mindful:
to be clear in vision, quick in hearing,
genial in expression, respectful in
demeanor, true in word, serious in
duty, inquiring in doubt, firmly self-
controlled in anger, just and fair
when the way to success lies open.

CONFUCIUS
The Analects

As is the characteristic of great minds to say much in few words, so, on the contrary, little minds have the gift of speaking much and saying little.

DUC FRANCOIS DE LA ROCHFOUCAULD
Maxims

A director should be correct. If you, as a leader, show correctness, who will dare not to be correct?

CONFUCIUS
The Analects

If you show dignity you will not be mocked; if you are indulgent you will win the multitude; if faithful, others will place their trust in you; if earnest, you will do something meritorious; and if kind, you will be enabled to avail yourself amply of the services of others.

CONFUCIUS
The Analects

Character is a natural power, like light and heat, and all nature cooperates with it. The reason why we feel one person's presence, and do not feel another's, is as simple as gravity... Character is the moral order seen through the medium of an individual nature.

RALPH WALDO EMERSON
Character

A perfect person is like a lotus leaf in
the water, or like a mud-fish in the
marsh. Neither of these is polluted
by the element in which it lives.

RAMAKRISHNA
The Gospel of Ramakrishna

The best of men is he who blushes
when you praise him and remains
silent when you defame him.

KAHLIL GIBRAN
Spiritual Sayings of Kahlil Gibran

The great depend on their heart, not on their purse. Genius and virtue, like diamonds, are best plain-set, set in lead, set in poverty. The greatest man in history was the poorest.

RALPH WALDO EMERSON
Character

It is the practice of the multitude to bark at eminent people, as little dogs do at strangers.

SENECA
Of a Happy Life, Ch. XIX

According to how you act, according to how you conduct yourself, so do you become. The person of good deeds becomes good. The person of evil deeds becomes evil. One becomes pure by virtuous action, bad by bad action.

UPANISHADS
(Hindu scripture)

"Well done, good and faithful servant!" said his master. "You have been
faithful in managing small amounts,
so I will put you in charge of large
amounts."

JESUS
Matthew 25:21 (TEV)

True eloquence consists in saying all
that is necessary, and nothing but
what is necessary.

DUC FRANCIS DE LA ROCHEFOUCAULD
Maxims

What the sages say
about beauty,
creativity,
and excellence

Though we travel the world over to find the beautiful, we must carry it with us, or we find it not... In the sculptures of the Greeks, in the masonry of the Romans, and in the pictures of the Tuscan and Venetian masters, the highest charm is the universal language they speak. A confession of moral nature, or purity, love, and hope breathes from them all. That which we carry to them, the same we bring back more fairly illustrated in the memory.

RALPH WALDO EMERSON
Character

In the elder days of Art,
Builders wrought with greatest care
Each minute and unseen part;
For the Gods see everywhere.

HENRY WADSWORTH LONGFELLOW
The Builders, St. 5

Doing easily what others find difficult is talent; doing what is impossi-
ble for talent is genius.

HENRI-FRÉDÉRIC AMIEL
Journal, Dec. 17, 1856

Nothing is good if it can be better.

SAINT AUGUSTINE
Confessions, XLI, 77.75

Workers who want to work well must first sharpen their tools.

CONFUCIUS
The Analects

If you be expert in any art, you need
not tell it, for your own skill will
show it.

SA'DI
The Gulistan

Excellence is an art won by training
and habituation; we do not act rightly
because we have virtue or excellence,
but we rather have these because we
have acted rightly; these virtues are
formed in us by our actions, we are
what we repeatedly do. Excellence,
then, is not an act but a habit: the

good of us is a working of the soul in the way of excellence in a complete life;... for as it is not one swallow or one fine day that makes a spring, so it is not one day or a short time that makes a person blessed and happy.

ARISTOTLE
Nicomachean Ethics

Many a genius has been slow of growth. Oaks that flourish for a thousand years do not spring up into beauty like a reed.

GEORGE HENRY LEWES
The Spanish Drama, Life of Lope de Vega, Ch. II

It is commonly said by farmers, that
a good pear or apple costs no more
time or pains to rear, than a poor one;
so I would have no work of art, no
speech, or action, or thought, or
friend, but the best.

RALPH WALDO EMERSON
Character

Genius is always ascetic; and piety
and love. Appetite shows to the finer
souls as a disease.

RALPH WALDO EMERSON
Character

As workers spend their time in their workshops for the perfecting of their work, so superior persons apply their minds to study in order to make themselves thoroughly conversant with their subjects.

CONFUCIUS
The Analects

What the sages say
about impermanence

Look upon the world as you would
on a bubble.

DHAMMAPADA
(Buddhist scripture) 13:170

So many love temporal things and
do not look for divine providence
which is the maker and governor of
time. Loving temporal things they
do not want the things they love to
pass away.

SAINT AUGUSTINE
Confessions, XXII, 42

I have put away my royal diadem;
and contrary to your way of thinking, I prefer, henceforth, no more to
rule. A hare rescued from the ser-
pent's mouth, would it go back again
to be devoured; holding a torch and
burning yourself, would you not let
it go? Would a blind person, on
recovering sight, again seek to be in
darkness?... You say that while
young a person should be gay and
when old then religious, but I regard
the feebleness of age as bringing with
it loss of power to be religious, unlike
the firmness and power of youth, the
will determined and the heart established;...

But I rejoice to have acquired religious wealth; if you say that I am young and tender, and that the time for seeking wisdom is not come, you ought to know that to seek true religion, there never is a time not fit; impermanence and fickleness, the hate of death, these ever follow us, and therefore I embrace the present day, convinced that now is the time to seek religion.

GAUTAMA
Life of Buddha

This only is the Law, that all things
are impermanent.

DHAMMAPADA
(Buddhist scripture) 20:277

The phenomena of life may be
likened unto a dream, a phantasm, a
bubble, a shadow, the glistening dew,
or lightning flash, and thus they
ought to be contemplated.

DIAMOND SUTRA
(Buddhist scripture)

What the sages say
about eternal values
and the pleasures of
this world

Blessed are the poor in spirit,
> for theirs is the kingdom of
> heaven.

Blessed are those who mourn
> for they shall be comforted.

Blessed are the meek
> for they shall inherit the earth.

Blessed are those who hunger and
> thirst for righteousness,
> for they shall be satisfied.

Blessed are the merciful
> for they shall obtain mercy.

Blessed are the pure in heart
> for they shall see God.

Blessed are the peacemakers
> for they shall be called children
> of God.

Blessed are those who are persecuted
for righteousness' sake,
for theirs is the kingdom of
heaven.

JESUS
Matthew 5:3–12

Like an image in a dream the world
is troubled by love, hatred, and other
poison. So long as the dream lasts,
the image appears to be real; but on
awaking it vanishes.

BHAGAVAD-GITA

Follow not after vanity, nor after the enjoyment of love and lust! The person who is earnest and meditative, obtains ample joy.

DHAMMAPADA
(Buddhist scripture) 2:27

The kingdom of God is within you.

JESUS
Luke 17:21 (KJV)

Do not love the world or anything that belongs to the world. If you love the world, you do not love God. Everything that belongs to the world – what the sinful self desires, what people see and want, and everything in this world that people are so proud of – none of this comes from God; it all comes from the world. The world and everything in it that people desire is passing away; but those who do the will of God live forever.

NEW TESTAMENT
1 John 2:15–17 (TEV)

Know that the life of this world is
only play, and idle talk, and pag-
eantry, and boasting among you, and
rivalry in respect of wealth and
children; as the likeness of vegetation
after rain, where the growth is pleas-
ing to the gardener, but afterward it
dries up and you see it turning
yellow, then it becomes straw.

KORAN
Surah 6

Go, sell what you own, and give the
money to the poor, and you will
have treasure in heaven; then come,
follow me.

JESUS
Mark 10:21 (NRSV)

When man invents a machine, he
runs it; then the machines begin to
run him, and he becomes the slave of
his slave.

KAHLIL GIBRAN
Spiritual Sayings of Kahlil Gibran

If you plant in the field of your natural desires, from it you will gather the harvest of death; if you plant in the field of the Spirit, from the Spirit you will gather the harvest of eternal life.

SAINT PAUL
Galatians 6:8 (TEV)

Do not be deceived; God is not mocked, for you reap whatever you sow.

SAINT PAUL
Galatians 6:7 (NRSV)

But lo! men have become the tools of their tools. The man who independently plucked the fruits when he was hungry is become a farmer; and he who stood under a tree for shelter, a housekeeper. We now no longer camp as for a night, but have settled down on earth and forgotten heaven... We have built for this world a family mansion, and for the next a family tomb.

HENRY DAVID THOREAU
Walden

The heavier scale of a balance goes
down while the lighter one rises up.
Similarly the person who is weighed
down with too many cares and
anxieties of the world goes down
into it, while the person who has
fewer cares rises up towards the
kingdom of heaven.

RAMAKRISHNA
The Gospel of Ramakrishna

Where, O death, is your victory?
Where, O death, where is your sting?

SAINT PAUL
1 Corinthians 15:55 (NRSV)

The person who submits to vanity,
and does not submit to meditation,
forgetting the real aim of life and
grasping at the pleasure, will in time
envy the person who has labored in
meditation.

DHAMMAPADA
(Buddhist scripture) 16:209

That which dwells within all living
bodies remains forever indestructible. Therefore, you should never
mourn for any one.

BHAGAVAD-GITA

If a person is tossed about by doubts, full of strong passions, and yearning only for what is delightful, their thirst will grow more and more, and they will indeed make their fetters strong.

DHAMMAPADA
(Buddhist scripture) 24:349

The Kingdom of heaven is like yeast. A woman takes it and mixes it with a bushel of flour, until the whole batch of dough rises.

JESUS
Matthew 13:33 (TEV)

The Kingdom of heaven is like this. A
person takes a mustard seed and sows
it in a field. It is the smallest of all
seeds, but when it grows up, it is the
biggest of all plants. It becomes a tree,
so that birds come and make their
nests in its branches.

JESUS
Matthew 13:31

True love transcends instantly the
unworthy object, and dwells and
broods on the eternal.

RALPH WALDO EMERSON
Character

The Kingdom of heaven is like this. A person happens to find a treasure hidden in a field. He covers it up again and is so happy that he goes and sells everything he has, and then goes back and buys the field.

JESUS
Matthew 13:44 (TEV)

Nothing divine dies. All good is eternally reproductive.

RALPH WALDO EMERSON
Character

Enter through the narrow gate; for
the gate is wide and the road is easy
that leads to destruction, and there
are many who take it. For the gate is
narrow and the road is hard that
leads to life, and there are few who
find it.

JESUS
Matthew 7:13–14, NRSV

When the morning's freshness has been replaced by the weariness of midday, when the leg muscles quiver under the strain, the climb seems endless, and, suddenly, nothing will go quite as you wish, it is then that you must not hesitate.

DAG HAMMARSKJÖLD
Markings

How soon may those who shout my
name today begin to revile it, because glory, and the memory of
people, and all things beside, are but
vanity – a sand heap under the
senseless wind, the barking of dogs,
the quarreling of children, weeping
incontinently upon their laughter.

MARCUS AURELIUS
Meditations

We must try to have a peaceful spirit. Our only escape is separation from worldly things. What I call flying from the world is not merely to separate one's self from it in body, but to detach all one's affections; to be without country, home, business, society, property; to be poor, unoccupied, unsociable, untaught in human sciences, prepared to receive in the heart the rules which spring from the divine teachings.

SAINT BASIL THE GREAT
Monastic Life, Vol. VII

A thousand years to you are like one
day; they are like yesterday, already
gone, like a short hour in the night.

HEBREW BIBLE / OLD TESTAMENT
Psalm 90:4 (TEV)

I have seen the business that God has
given to everyone to be busy with.
God has made everything suitable
for its time; moreover God has put
eternity into their minds.

HEBREW BIBLE / OLD TESTAMENT
Ecclesiastes 3:10–11

In accumulating property for ourselves or our posterity, in founding a
family or a state, or acquiring fame
even, we are mortal; but in dealing
with truth we are immortal, and
need fear no change nor accident.

HENRY DAVID THOREAU
Walden

I saw Eternity the other night
Like a great ring of pure and endless
light.

HENRY VAUGHAN
The World

That Reality which pervades the universe is indestructible. No one has power to change the Changeless. Bodies are said to die, but That which possesses the body is eternal. It cannot be limited, or destroyed.

BHAGAVAD-GITA

As for us, our life is like grass. We grow and flourish like a wild flower; then the wind blows on it, and it is gone – no one sees it again.

HEBREW BIBLE / OLD TESTAMENT
Psalm 103:15–16 (TEV)

When all desires that dwell in the
heart cease, then the mortal becomes
immortal, and obtains Brahman.
When all the ties of the heart are
severed here on earth, then the
mortal becomes immortal.

UPANISHADS
(Hindu scripture)

Realize that pleasure and pain, gain
and loss, victory and defeat, are all
one and the same.

BHAGAVAD-GITA

The truly wise mourn neither for the living nor for the dead. There was never a time when I did not exist, nor you, nor any of these kings. Nor is there any future in which we shall cease to be.

Just as the dweller in this body passes through childhood, youth and old age, so at death we merely pass into another kind of body. The wise are not deceived by that.

Feelings of heat and cold, pleasure and pain, are caused by the contact of the senses with their objects. They come and they go, never lasting long. You must accept them.

A serene spirit accepts pleasure and pain with an even mind, and is unmoved by either. That spirit alone is worthy of immortality.

That which is non-existent can never come into being, and that which is can never cease to be. Those who have known the inmost Reality know also the nature of IS and IS NOT.

UPANISHADS
(Hindu scripture)

I am a part of all that I have met.

ALFRED, LORD TENNYSON
Ulysses, L.18

To every thing there is a season,
    and a time to every purpose
    under the heaven;
A time to be born, and a time to die;
    a time to plant,
    and a time to pluck up that which
    is planted;
A time to kill, and a time to heal;
    a time to break down,
    and a time to build up;
A time to weep, and a time to laugh;
    a time to mourn,
    and a time to dance;
A time to cast away stones, and a time
    to gather stones together;
    a time to embrace, and a time
    to refrain from embracing;

A time to get, and a time to lose;

    a time to keep,

    and a time to cast away;

A time to rend, and a time to sew;

    a time to keep silence,

    and a time speak;

A time to love, and a time to hate;

    a time of war, and a time of

    peace.

HEBREW BIBLE / OLD TESTAMENT
Ecclesiastes 3:1–8(KJV)

A generation goes, and a generation comes, but the earth remains forever. The sun rises and the sun goes down, and hastens to where it rises. The wind blows to the south, and goes round to the north; round and round goes the wind, and on its circuits the wind returns. All streams run to the sea, but the sea is not full; to the place where the streams flow, there they flow again. All things are full of weariness; one cannot utter it; the eye is not satisfied with seeing, nor the ear filled with hearing. What has been is what will be, and what has been done is what will be done; and there is nothing new under the sun.

HEBREW BIBLE / OLD TESTAMENT
Ecclesiastes 1:4–9

Far, far will I go,
Far away beyond the high hills,
Where the birds live,
Far away over yonder, far away over
yonder.

Two pieces of rock barred the way,
Two mighty rocks,
That opened and closed
Like a pair of jaws.
There was no way past,
One must go in between them
To reach the land beyond and away
Beyond the high hills,
The birds' land.

Two land bears barred the way,
Two land bears fighting

And barring the way.

There was no road,

And yet I would gladly pass on and

away

To the farther side of the high hills,

To the birds' land.

INUIT
from Knud Rasmussen, Beyond the High Hills

If I have got to drag my trap, I will take care that it be a light one and does not nip me in a vital part. But perchance it would be wisest never to put one's paw into it.

HENRY DAVID THOREAU
Walden

The Golden Rule

A certain heathen came to Shammai and said to him, "Make me a proselyte, on condition that you teach me the whole Torah while I stand on one foot." Thereupon he repulsed him with the rod which was in his hand. When he went to Hillel, he said to him, "What is hateful to you, do not do to your neighbor: that is the whole Torah; all the rest of it is commentary; go and learn."

TALMUD
Shabbat 31a

Try your best to treat others as you
would wish to be treated yourself,
and you will find that this is the
shortest way to benevolence.

MENCIUS
VII.A.4

One should not behave towards
others in a way which is disagreeable
to oneself. This is the essence of
morality. All other activities are due
to selfish desire.

MAHABHARATA
Anusasana Parva 113.8

Do not unto others what you would
not have them do unto you.

CONFUCIUS
The Analects

Do not say, "I will do to others as
they have done to me; I will pay
them back for what they have done."

HEBREW BIBLE / OLD TESTAMENT
Proverbs 24:29 (NRSV)

In everything, do to others as you
would have them do to you; for this
is the law of the prophets.

JESUS
Matthew 7:12 (NRSV)

About the Sages
quoted

ADDISON, JOSEPH (1672–1719). English essayist, poet, and man of letters.

AMIEL, HENRI FRÉDÉRIC (1821–1888). A Swiss professor whose *Journal* has come to be seen as one of the great biographies.

ARISTOTLE (284–322 BCE). Greek philosopher whose works encompass metaphysics, mathematics, physics, biology, logic, ethics, politics, and the scientific method.

BACON FRANCIS (1561–1626). Philosopher, essayist, and Lord Chancellor of England.

BENEDICTINE MONKS (c. 480–553 c.e.). An order of monks who follow the Rule of St. Benedict of Nursia.

CARLYLE, THOMAS (1795–1881).
British essayist and historian.

CATO, DIONYSIUS. He is believed to
have written a famous book of maxims in the third or fourth century, CE.

CHUANG-TZU (died 272 BCE) was a
Taoist social reformer and through his
writings Taoism became popular.

CICERO, MARCUS TULLIUS (106–43
BCE). Great Roman orator and politi-
cian, student of law and philosophy
and writer of letters.

CONFUCIUS (551–479 BCE). A
famous Chinese philosopher.

CONGREVE, WILLIAM (1670–1729).
Restoration dramatist famed for his
witty contributions to the comedy of
manners. A friend of Swift, Steele,
and Pope.

DE LA ROCHFOUCALD, DUC
FRANCOIS VI (1613–1680). French
author known for his *Maxims* (1664–
1665) which are written in a lucid and
concise style.

DISRAELI, BENJAMIN (1804–1881).
English novelist and statesman, prime
minister in 1868 and 1874–1880.

EDDY, MARY BAKER (1821–1910).
American religious figure, founder and
leader of the Christian Science movement. Based on spiritual healing, she
evolved a new system of religious
philosophy, as recorded in the book
Science and Health. She founded the
Church of Christ, Scientist, and
established several journals including
the *Christian Science Monitor*.

ELIOT, GEORGE (1819–1880). The pen name for the English writer Mary Ann Evans. One of the principal novelists of the 19th century, she was opposed to organized religion and was criticized for her irregular association with George Henry Lewes.

EMERSON, RALPH WALDO (1803–1882). American poet and essayist, one of the founders of Transcendentalism. Influenced Thoreau, Whitman, and Emily Dickinson.

EPICTETUS (c. 60–40 CE) A stoic philosopher whose teachings were recorded by his pupil, Arrian, in two works: *Discourses* and *The Manual.* Originally a slave, Epictetus obtained his freedom and conducted a philosophic school. He had great faith in the government of the world by an all-wise Providence. He summed up the basis of his teaching in two words, "endure" and "abstain."

FIELDS, JAMES T. (1817–1881).
American publisher and author.

FRANKLIN, BENJAMIN (1706–1790).
American printer, statesman and
writer, said to have "invented the
Hoax, the Lightning Rod, and the
Republic."

FRIEDAN, BETTY Contemporary
American writer whose work influ-
enced the Women's Liberation
Movement.

FROUDE, JAMES ANTHONY (1818–
1894). English historian.

GAUTAMA, SIDDHARTHA (c. 600
BCE). Name of religious reformer who
came to be recognized as the Buddha
(the "enlightened"), hence the name
Buddhism given to the faith he
founded.

GIBRAN, KAHLIL (1883–1931).
Lebanese-born Syrian-American
symbolist poet, spiritual writer, and
painter, who combined Oriental and
Occidental ideas. His funeral in 1931
was attended by religious leaders from
many faiths.

GRAHAM, BILLY. Contemporary
American evangelist.

HAMMARSKJÖLD, DAG (1905–
1961). Born in Sweden in 1905.
Elected Secretary General of the
United Nations in 1953 and again in
1957. While in office, he died in a
plane crash in 1961 in Rhodesia.
Markings is a book of his spiritual
reflections that was discovered and
published after his death.

HERBERT, GEORGE (1593–1633).
English poet and Anglican clergyman,
best known for his poems in *The
Temple*. *Jacula Prudentum* is a collection of wise sayings.

JAMES, WILLIAM (1842–1910)
American psychologist and
philosopher.

JESUS OF NAZARETH (c. 1–30 CE).
Jewish religious teacher recognized by
his followers as the "Christ" (Greek for
Jewish word "Messiah") and venerated
by Christians as the Second Person of
the Divine Trinity.

JOHNSON, SAMUEL (1709–1784).
English poet, critic, and man of letters
whose *Dictionary* (1755) was an
innovation in its time. His fascinating
and eccentric personality was de-
scribed by James Boswell in his *Life of
Johnson*.

LEWES, GEORGE HENRY (1817–1878). English philosopher and critic.

LOCKE, JOHN (1632–1704). English philosopher who translated the sayings in this collection from the Latin of Juvenal (50–130 CE).

LONGFELLOW, HENRY WADSWORTH (1807–1882). American poet and university teacher.

LUTHER, MARTIN (1483–1546). German religious reformer, professor of biblical exegesis at Wittenberg, who set in motion the Protestant Reformation by his attacks on the contemporary doctrines underlying many religious practices. Luther translated the Bible into German, wrote hymns and many theological treatises. The Lutheran church is named for him.

MANN, HORACE (1796–1859).
American educator and statesman.

MARCUS AURELIUS (121–180 CE).
Roman emperor who wrote *Meditations*, a collection of stoic reflections on life.

MILTON, JOHN (1608–1674). English Puritan poet, one of the most respected figures in English literature. Best known for his biblical epics *Paradise Lost* and *Paradise Regained*.

MONTAIGNE, MICHEL DE (1533–1595). French nobleman, soldier, and lawyer. Highly educated, he wrote his personal observations in his *Essays* (1582, 1587, 1588) which had a wide influence in England.

MORMON RELIGION. The correct name for this group is The Church of Jesus Christ of Latter Day Saints. It was organized in the United States in 1830 by Joseph Smith. *Doctrine and Covenants* is one of the four scriptures; the other three are *The Book of Mormon, The Bible* (Old and New Testaments), and *The Pearl of Great Price.*

MO-TI (born c. 500 BCE). A Chinese sage, younger contemporary of Confucius and critic of the Confucian system. Founder of a religion, comparable to Christianity and Buddhism, in which love played a central role.

NEEDHAM, RICHARD. Modern writer, was a columnist for the T*oronto Globe and Mail.*

OSLER, SIR WILLIAM (1849–1919).
Famous Canadian physician and
educator, he also won distinction in
the United States and England.

PITT, WILLIAM (Earl of Chatham)
(1708–1778). English statesman,
prime minister for many years. Called
Pitt the Elder to distinguish him from
his son of the same name who also
became prime minister.

POPE, ALEXANDER (1688–1744).
English poet, dominant literary figure
of his time. His work is characterized
by technical finish, epigrammatic
form, and satire. Possibly most quoted
poet in English after Shakespeare.

PTAH-HOTEP (c. 2450 BCE). A
collection of pieces of advice for state
officials collected together under the
name of Ptah-Hotep, vizier of one of
the early kings of Egypt.

PYTHAGORAS (born c. 580 BCE)
Founder of a philosophical school. He
was interested in the doctrine of the
transmigration of the soul and the
mathematical nature of philosophical
truth.

RAMAKRISHNA (1836–1886). Title
adopted by Gadadhar Chatterji, a
Hindu holy man and teacher.
Preached the essential unity behind
all religions.

RASMUSSEN, KNUD JOHAN VIC-
TOR (1879–1933). Danish arctic
explorer and ethnologist.

ROOSEVELT, THEODORE (1858–
1919). Twenty-sixth president of the
United States.

RUSKIN, JOHN (1819–1900). English
painter, art critic, and writer known
for his rebellion against the materialis-
tic standards of his age.

SA'DI (1184–1291 CE). The most popular Persian poet, author of *Gulistan* (*The Rose Garden*, 1258).

SAINT AUGUSTINE (354–430 CE). One of greatest thinkers of the patristic church. He is regarded by some as the first modern man because of his interest in and insight into human psychology.

SAINT BASIL THE GREAT (died 379 CE). Influential monastic writer of the Eastern church whose best-known works were derived from questions put to him by monastic communities.

SAINT PAUL (c. 1–66 CE) Important apostle in the early Christian church. His teachings are recorded in his letters to the Christian communities he founded during his missionary travels. These letters are probably the oldest documents in the New Testament.

SANTAYANA, GEORGE (1863–1952). Spanish-born American author and philosopher, educated at Harvard.

SCHOPENHAUER, ARTHUR (1788–1860). German philosopher who emphasized the will to live as the fundamental reality and the cause of suffering.

SENECA (c. 4 BCE–65 CE) Roman statesman and philosopher.

SEWARD, WILLIAM HENRY (1801–1872). An American statesman known for being a strong opponent of slavery.

SPINOZA, BARUCH (or Benedictus) (1632–1677). Influential philosopher in the modern European tradition. Born of Jewish parents in Holland, but later expelled from the synagogue. Accused of atheism in his own day, but later regarded by the Romantic movement as "a God-intoxicated man."

TENNYSON, ALFRED LORD (1809–1892). One of the greatest of the Victorian poets and certainly, in his own day, one of the most popular. Appointed poet laureate in 1850.

THOREAU, HENRY DAVID (1817–1862). American naturalist, philosopher, and writer.

VAUGHAN, HENRY (1622–1695). British poet.

WESLEY, JOHN (1703–1791). An English preacher strongly influenced by German pietism. Founder of Methodism.

About the religious
scriptures quoted

In this collection, texts have been chosen which are self-explanatory. However, since some may wish to follow up with further reading, here are a few words about the various religious documents cited.

For the sake of simplicity, the generic word scripture has been used to describe a writing considered important by any religion. It should be pointed out that the status of sacred books varies from religion to religion.

Buddhism: The traditions about the life and teachings of Gautama were transmitted orally for about four centuries before being committed to writing. The Buddhist scriptures in the Tripitaka (etymologically and actually "the three baskets") are very extensive. The *Dhammapada* is a collection of verses on the law.

Confucianism: Named for Confucius, a learned sage who traveled a great deal. Ironically, at his death, he felt he had failed, although his teachings came to have a formative influence on Chinese society. His sayings were recorded long after his death and there are problems of authenticity.

Other Chinese sages quoted: Mencius was the systematizer (and some would argue perverter) of Confucian doctrine. Lao-Tzu is a representative of Taoism, the other great indigenous Chinese religion. The influence of Mo-ti, who in fact provided a third alternative to Confucian and Taoist thought, did not persevere in China.

Judaism and Christianity: Both these faiths share the book called respectively the *Hebrew Bible* or the *Old Testament*. Protestants generally accept the same books in the canon (i.e. the list of books that belong) as Jews. A further collection of books known as the Apocrypha is included by the Roman Catholic Church in its Old Testament. Many Protestant Bibles nonetheless include this collection in a separate section called *The Apocrypha* separate from the Old and New Testaments.

In Judaism the *Talmud* is very important. It is made up of the *Mishnah*, a collection of oral laws and sayings collected about 100 c.e., and the Gemara which is nominally a commentary on the *Mishnah* but which, in fact, includes a great deal of material only loosely connected to the *Mishnah*. There are two *Talmuds*: the Babylonian, which is the more important, and the Jerusalem, which is a much smaller work.

In Christianity, the Bible includes both the Old and New Testaments. The New Testament is centered around the life, teachings, and importance of Jesus of Nazareth recognized as the Messiah (*Christos* in Greek, hence "Christ" and "Christian.")

Hinduism: The number and variety of Hindu scriptures is not easily discussed. The works cited in this book are the *Laws of Manu* (a document describing the general rules of life for all Hindus of whatever caste), some of the *Puranas* (scriptures more readily available to the general public), the *Hitopadesa* (a collection of folk tales), and the *Bhagavad-Gita* (a much-loved book which is in fact a small section in the much – very much – larger epic the *Mahabharata*).

Islam: Mohammed was the great prophet of Islam. About 600 c.e. he proclaimed a strict monotheistic faith which, while it accepts the Hebrew Bible and New Testament as revelations of God, has as its central document the Koran revealed to Mohammed.

Sikhism: A religion with roots in Hinduism, it was founded by Guru Nanak who was born in 1469. While opinions differ about Sikhism's debt to other faiths, its adherents see it as an independent movement. The scriptures of Sikhism are called the *Guru Granth Sahib* or *Adi Granth*.

Zoroastrianism: Founded by the prophet Zoroaster (sixth century b.c.e.), a native of Persia. Zoroastrianism was a monotheistic religion which dominated the Persian Empire between the sixth century b.c.e and the fourth century c.e. It survives solely among some 100,000 Parsees of India and some scattered remnants in Iran. Its sacred scriptures, called the *Avesta*, exist in a fragmentary state.